Escape to Freedom

ESCAPE TO FREEDOM

Sometimes I feel like sitting some place very quiet, and taking my hat off, and thinking the biggest thoughts I can think about Frederick Douglass—such a giant of a person was he, both in his own life and in the history of black people. Fred—were he alive today—would be about one hundred and sixty-two years old; but he is still one of the most modern and up-to-date Americans I know . . . my hero . . . my role model.

A man's books are not altogether unlike children. He brings them forth, tries to give them character and substance and personality—to make them as important to his readers as to himself; yet in the end, a book has to live its own life. Once Papa has launched it out into the mainstream, he can only stand on the sidelines, keep track, and wish it well. *Escape to Freedom*, the story of the boyhood of Frederick Douglass, has already made me proud and fatherly. And the fact that it now goes into a second printing indicates that there are others out there who have the same bubbling-up feelings I have about Frederick Douglass; how he swapped bread with little white boys, because he was hungry for what was more important—the knowledge in their schoolbooks. How, in spite of the fact that it was against the law, he sneaked behind the backs of the people who owned him, and taught himself to read and write. How knowledge made Fred rebellious, and he was sent to a special plantation to be broken and tamed like a mule; but where—risking his life—he battled the vicious slave breaker blow for blow, and finally whipped him! And how, after forging his own pass, and pretending to be a sailor, he got on the train as bold as you please and made his escape from Baltimore to freedom. This has to be one of the most exciting stories an American boy or girl could read—and every word of it true!

If Frederick Douglass were alive today I am sure the president would appoint him head of all the boards of education in the country, especially the drop out department. I have no doubt, drawing on his own childhood, he would talk to the students as only one of America's greatest orators could talk—weaving such magnificent stories, right out of his own life—that they would sit there—as completely caught as I am, even now, whenever I think about the man; for they, too, would see what an exciting, hair-raising, breathtaking, high-flying adventure getting an education can be! If, with this book I can share with them the smallest part of what I felt when I was a boy, and first read about Fred, and his fantastic escape to freedom, and how it opened a whole new universe for me, then . . . WOW!

Ossie Davis
New Rochelle, New York
July 1989

Escape to Freedom

A PLAY ABOUT
YOUNG FREDERICK DOUGLASS

OSSIE DAVIS

PUFFIN BOOKS

PUFFIN BOOKS

A Division of Penguin Books USA Inc.

375 Hudson Street, New York, New York 10014

Penguin Books Ltd, 27 Wrights Lane, London W8 5TZ, England

Penguin Books Australia Ltd, Ringwood, Victoria, Australia

Penguin Books Canada Ltd, 10 Alcorn Avenue, Toronto, Ontario, Canada M4V 3B2

Penguin Books (N.Z.) Ltd, 182-190 Wairau Road, Auckland 10, New Zealand

Penguin Books Ltd, Registered Offices: Harmondsworth, Middlesex, England

First published in the United States of America by Viking Penguin,
a division of Penguin Books USA Inc., 1978
Published in Puffin Books, 1990
21 23 25 27 29 30 28 26 24 22
Copyright © Ossie Davis, 1976
All rights reserved

Caution: Professionals and amateurs are hereby warned that *Escape to Freedom* is
subject to a royalty. It is fully protected under the copyright laws of the United
States of America, the British Commonwealth, including the Dominion of Canada,
and all other countries of the Copyright Union. All rights, including professional,
amateur, motion pictures, recitation, lecturing, public reading, radio broadcasting,
television, and the rights of translation into foreign languages, are strictly reserved.

In its present form the play is dedicated to the reading public only.

Particular emphasis is laid on the question of amateur performances or stock
performances, inclusive of readings, permission and terms for which must be
secured in writing from Samuel French, Inc., at 45 West 25th Street, New York,
N.Y. 10010, or at 7623 Sunset Boulevard, Hollywood, California 90046, or to
Samuel French (Canada) Ltd., 80 Richmond Street East, Toronto, Ontario,
Canada M5C 1P1.

For all other rights than those stipulated above, apply to Marian Searchinger As-
sociates, Inc., at 327 Central Park West, New York, N.Y. 10025.

Copying from this book in whole or in part is strictly forbidden by law.

LIBRARY OF CONGRESS CATALOGING IN PUBLICATION DATA

Davis, Ossie.   Escape to freedom : a play about young Frederick Douglass / Ossie Davis.   p.   cm.
Summary: Born a slave, young Frederick Douglass endures many years
of cruelty before escaping to the North to claim his freedom.
ISBN 0-14-034355-5
1. Douglass, Frederick, 1817?–1895—Juvenile drama.   2. Slavery—
United States—Juvenile drama.   [1. Douglass, Frederick, 1817?–1895—Drama.
2. Afro-Americans—Drama.   3. Slavery—Drama.   4. Plays.]   I. Title.
[PS3507.A7444E84 1990]   812'.54—dc20   89-36937

Printed in the United States of America
Set in Caledonia

Except in the United States of America, this book is sold subject to the condition
that it shall not, by way of trade or otherwise, be lend, re-sold, hired out, or
otherwise circulated without the publisher's prior consent in any form of binding or
cover other than that which it is published and without a similar condition
including this condition being imposed on the subsequent purchaser.

R0430263959

THE TIME
The 1830s

THE PLACE
*The Eastern Shore of Maryland,
and Baltimore*

CAST OF CHARACTERS
Fred Douglass
Black Woman
Black Man
Black Boy
White Woman
White Man
White Boy

NOTE:
All the actors indicated above may play the
various parts as indicated, except in the case of
Fred Douglass.

Escape to Freedom, by Ossie Davis, directed by Robbie McCauley, with musical arrangements and direction by Harrison Fisher, was first presented by Performing Arts Repertory Theatre (P.A.R.T.) at Town Hall, New York City, on March 8, 1976.

CAST

Frederick Douglass	*Jesse Goins*
Black Boy	*Myles McMillan*
Black Man	*John Henry Redwood*
Black Woman	*Mimi Ayers*
White Woman	*Lynn Kearney*
White Boy	*Stephen Scott*
White Man	*John McNamara*

Prologue

[*Curtain rises to reveal entire cast on stage as song begins.*]

COMPANY

> I'm on my way (my way)
> To the freedom land (freedom land)
> I'm on my way, great God
> I'm on my way
> I'm on my way
> To the freedom land

[COMPANY *hums melody under narration.*]

FRED [*To audience*] My name is Frederick Douglass. I was born a slave, near Easton, in Talbot County, Maryland, in 1817 or 1818—I never knew which.

BLACK WOMAN   This book—a narrative of the life of Frederick Douglass—this little book, and the man who wrote it, helped millions of Americans to make up their minds that it was an evil thing to hold black people—or any people—in slavery.

[BLACK WOMAN *exits.*]

WHITE BOY   To tell our story, each of us will change his costume from time to time . . .

BLACK MAN   And become different characters when it is necessary.

[WHITE BOY *and* BLACK MAN *exit.*]

WHITE MAN   All except one—the young man who will play the part of Frederick Douglass.

[WHITE MAN, WHITE WOMAN, *and* BLACK BOY *exit.* FRED *crosses to center stage as the rest of the stage lights fade to half.*]

Scene One

[*A slave cabin. Behind* FRED, *we see* BLACK WOMAN *enter with candle and kneel beside a dummy baby—young* FRED—*wrapped in a gunny sack and lying on the floor.*]

FRED   [*To audience*] My mother's name was Harriet Bailey. I took the name Douglass later in my life. I never saw my mother more than four or five times in my life, and each time was very brief—and always at night.

[BLACK WOMAN *picks up baby and begins singing softly as she rocks it to sleep.* FRED *continues narration under song.*]

BLACK WOMAN

      Black sheep, black sheep
      Where'd you lose your lamb?

Way down in the valley
The birds and the butterflies
Are picking out its eyes
Poor little thing crying mammy
Go and tell Aunt Susie
Go and tell Aunt Susie
Go and tell Aunt Susie
The old gray goose is dead.

FRED   She did not live with me, but was hired out by my master to a man who lived about twelve miles down the road, which she had to walk, at night, after she was through working, in order to see me at all. She couldn't stay long, being a field hand—the penalty for not showing up in the fields at sunrise was a severe whipping. It was whispered that my master was my father, but my mother, in the few times I ever got to see her, never told me one way or another.

[BLACK WOMAN *puts baby back on the floor, covers it with a gunny sack, takes one last look, and exits.*]

FRED   Long before I waked she would be gone. After my mother died I was sent to live with my Aunt Jenny, but we had almost no time at all to be together. I was one of three or four hundred slaves who lived on the plantation. I was not old enough to work in the fields —I was only about seven at the time. I had no bed, no regular place to sleep, and would probably have died from hunger and cold, except that on the coldest nights I would steal a sack that was used for carrying corn to the mill, and crawl into it, and go to sleep on the cold, damp floor.

6

[FRED *finds a gunny sack, crawls into it, and tries to cover up for the night, but he is too tall and his feet stick out of the bottom. He tries to find a more comfortable position and finally goes to sleep. A beat, to indicate passage of time. A sudden noise and a light bursting through the door bring* FRED *awake.* WHITE BOY, *as overseer, bursts in, followed by* BLACK BOY, *as a very frightened young slave.* WHITE BOY, *seeing* FRED *asleep, pushes him with his foot.*]

WHITE BOY   Where is she, boy—where is your Aunt Jenny?

FRED   [*Scared out of his wits, trying to pull himself together, trying to wake up*] Where is who, sir?

WHITE BOY   [*Snatching* FRED *to his feet*] Don't mess with me, boy, you know who I mean! I'm talking about your Aunt Jenny—now, where did she go when she left here last night?

FRED   [*Completely in the dark*] My Aunt Jenny wasn't here last night—

[WHITE BOY *turns to* BLACK BOY, *standing nearby, as* WHITE MAN *and* BLACK WOMAN *enter.*]

BLACK BOY   That's what she told us when she left the cabin last night, Mr. Gore—said she was coming over here to say good night to Frederick, her nephew—

FRED   I ain't seen my Aunt Jenny since a long, long time ago—

WHITE BOY   You lie to me, boy, and I'll break your neck.

7

FRED   I ain't lying, Mr. Gore, I ain't lying!

WHITE MAN   [*As Colonel Lloyd, to* BLACK BOY] You know what happens to darkies who try to escape from me, don't you?

BLACK BOY   Yessir—

WHITE MAN   Was your Aunt Jenny in here to see you last night? Tell me the truth—

FRED   I am telling the truth, Colonel Lloyd—my Aunt Jenny wasn't here last night.

[WHITE MAN, *satisfied, turns from* FRED. WHITE BOY, *not to be outdone, turns to the other slaves.*]

WHITE BOY   Well, if she didn't come here, she must have run away, and if she ran away, she must have had some help—now, who did it? Which one of you lazy, shiftless no-goods helped Jenny escape?

[BLACK WOMAN *and* BLACK BOY, *afraid of what they know is coming, ad-lib their earnest denials.*]

BLACK WOMAN *and* BLACK BOY   Please, sir, Mr. Gore, we ain't done nothing! It wasn't me, sir! We don't know nothing!

[BLACK MAN *hurries in.*]

BLACK MAN   Colonel Lloyd! Colonel Lloyd, sir—

WHITE MAN   What is it, Jethro?

BLACK MAN   It's Uncle Noah, sir—

WHITE MAN   Uncle Noah? What about him?

8

BLACK MAN   Uncle Noah's done escaped, too!

WHITE BOY   Oh, my God! They're running off together!

[WHITE BOY *and* WHITE MAN *race off. The three blacks wait until they are sure they are not being observed, then they jump up and down in glee as they celebrate the fact.* FRED *watches, not fully understanding, until he finally manages to get* BLACK MAN'S *attention.*]

FRED   Uncle Jethro! Uncle Jethro—why you-all dancing?

BLACK MAN   [*Trying to keep his voice down*] We celebrating the escape! Jenny and Noah, they done escaped —and we celebrating! If they makes it and don't get caught, it means they *free!* No more having to call some mean old white man your master—

[BLACK MAN *looks around and is suddenly aware that* WHITE MAN *and* WHITE BOY *are at the door and within earshot.* BLACK MAN *grabs* FRED *by the head and pushes him to his knees.* BLACK BOY *and* BLACK WOMAN, *catching on, sink to their knees also.* BLACK MAN *looks upward to heaven as if what follows were a continuation of heartfelt prayer.*]

BLACK MAN   Master, master, oh, gracious master, look down from your throne of grace and mercy and catch ol' Noah and Jenny by the scruffs of their no-good necks—

WHITE BOY   All right, that's enough of that bull—

BLACK MAN   I was just trying to help Colonel Lloyd in this deep, dark hour of his distress—

WHITE BOY   Enough, I say—and get out of here, the lot of you, and get into them fields and get to work—now! [*Indicating* FRED] Not you, boy.

[BLACK MAN, BLACK WOMAN, *and* BLACK BOY *hurry out.* WHITE BOY *turns to* WHITE MAN, *indicating* FRED.]

WHITE BOY   Colonel, you want me to send this boy to the fields with the rest of them?

WHITE MAN   No. All I want from Fred is that he looks after my yard—my flowers, my trees, and my fruit—right, boy?

FRED   Yes, sir.

[WHITE MAN *and* WHITE BOY *exit.* FRED *is left alone.* BLACK BOY *and* WHITE WOMAN *enter, as trees in the orchard. They are carrying prop trees, which* FRED *eyes hungrily.*]

FRED   [*To audience*] This garden was not the least source of trouble on the plantation. Its excellent fruit was quite a temptation to the hungry swarm of boys, as well as the older slaves. Scarcely a day passed but that some slave had to take the lash for stealing fruit.

[FRED *crosses to one tree and tries to shake loose an apple; no luck. He moves to the other tree and shakes it; an apple falls. He grabs the apple, looks around, and starts offstage as* BLACK MAN *enters and grabs him.*]

BLACK MAN   Gotcha!

FRED   [*Struggling to free himself*] Let me go—let me go!

BLACK MAN   [*Laughing, but still hanging on*] Stealing the Colonel's apples—how about that?

FRED   Please, Jethro, let me go!

[BLACK MAN *looks around to see if anyone is looking. Satisfied that the two of them are alone, he lets* FRED *loose.*]

BLACK MAN   Colonel catch you stealing his apples, he skin you, boy—

FRED   I know, Jethro, but I'm hungry—are you gonna tell?

BLACK MAN   There's only one way I know to get you out of this mess, boy, and save your thieving hide.

FRED   What's that?

BLACK MAN   Consume the evidence, boy—consume the evidence!

[BLACK MAN *takes a huge bite out of the apple and passes the remainder to* FRED.]

FRED   Where you been, Jethro?

BLACK MAN   [*Grinning as he eats*] Where you think I been, boy?

FRED   [*Excited at the prospect*] Baltimore! You been to Baltimore!

BLACK MAN   [*Pride of accomplishment*] Right! Boy, you ought to see that place!

11

[*An angry voice from offstage startles them.*]

BLACK WOMAN   [*Offstage*] Fred! Where you at, boy?

[BLACK MAN *pulls* FRED *down and ducks himself just as* BLACK WOMAN *hurries on, carrying a clean shirt.*]

BLACK WOMAN   [*Looking around*] Fred—boy, you're gonna get a whipping if you don't watch out!

[BLACK WOMAN *exits. When the coast is clear,* BLACK MAN *and* FRED *raise their heads again.*]

FRED   I better git—

[FRED *starts to rise, but* BLACK MAN *pulls him back down.*]

BLACK MAN   But I ain't told you what all I seen in Baltimore!

[*Much as* FRED *wants to leave, he cannot give up a chance to hear more.*]

FRED   What did you see in Baltimore, Jethro?

BLACK MAN   I'll tell you—but only if you promise: every time you shake down some of Colonel Lloyd's apples or oranges or whatnot, you save some for me.

FRED   [*Hesitates, then takes the plunge.*] I'll do it, Jethro, I'll do it—now tell me—

BLACK MAN   Well, first, there's the streets, wide, long, and all laid out—and on either side, houses to put them to shame.

FRED   Do the slaves live in houses?

12

BLACK MAN   Of course they do! They wear shoes—

FRED   [*Astounded*] They wear shoes!

BLACK MAN   Sometimes—and warm clothes, and sometimes even hats.

FRED   Hats? Even when they work in the fields?

BLACK MAN   [*Scornful*] Ain't no fields in Baltimore, boy— Baltimore is a city, a great big city. All the slaves there work as house servants, with plenty to eat and drink all the time.

FRED   [*Dreaming*] I sure wish I could go to Baltimore!

BLACK MAN   [*Expanding*] And that ain't all. Guess what else I seen?

FRED   What, Jethro?

BLACK MAN   I seen a black man—who was free.

FRED   [*Not quite grasping the concept*] Free? You saw a black man who owned himself?

BLACK MAN   Yeah—he was a sailor.

[BLACK WOMAN *enters and spots the two.*]

BLACK WOMAN   So there you are, both of you—stealing master's fruit!

BLACK MAN   Uh. Uh! [BLACK MAN *and* FRED *jump up.*] We ain't stealing. Hard as we work for Colonel Lloyd— and for nothing—we deserve this fruit! It's part of our pay!

BLACK WOMAN   Good. I'm sure Colonel Lloyd will be glad to hear that.

BLACK MAN   [*Giving up*] Aw, woman—come on, Fred.

[BLACK MAN *and* FRED *start off*.]

BLACK WOMAN   No, you don't, Fred Bailey—I got a message from the master.

[BLACK MAN *exits*. FRED *turns to* BLACK WOMAN.]

FRED   What message?

BLACK WOMAN   First, you're to take off that filthy shirt—then you're to scrub yourself with soap and water and get into these clean clothes.

FRED   What for?

BLACK WOMAN   You're going to Baltimore—

FRED   Baltimore!

BLACK WOMAN   Master's nephew and his wife need somebody to help look after the house and their little boy. Well, don't stand there gawking, boy, get into this shirt!

[FRED *grins and starts immediately to take off his shirt as* "Bright Glory" *song begins offstage*.]

Scene Two

[*While singing "Bright Glory," the cast changes the set to an arrangement suggesting a neat back yard, with a white picket fence, a table, and a chair. On the table is a Bible and a plate of buttered bread.*]

COMPANY

> *You don't hear me praying here*
> *You can't find me nowhere (can't find me)*
> *Come on up to bright glory*
> *I'll be waiting up there*
> *I'll be waiting up there, my Lord*
> *I'll be waiting up there (be waiting)*
> *Come on up to bright glory*
> *I'll be waiting up there.*

[COMPANY *continues to hum melody offstage as dialogue continues.*]

[FRED *and* JETHRO *enter.* FRED *is carrying a small bundle. They cross into yard.*]

JETHRO   Well, Frederick, here we are.

FRED   [*Looking around, taking it all in*] Baltimore.

JETHRO   [*Pointing*] And that's the house, right over there. Now, remember, mind your manners; show Mr. and Mrs. Auld what a good little nigger you are—no sass, no back talk, remember your place. Keep your head bowed and your eyes on the ground—and whatever they tell you to do—do it! Right away—understand?

FRED   Yes, Jethro, but—do what?

[*Humming offstage ends.*]

JETHRO   Don't worry, they'll tell you. Now I got to be going—

FRED   But ain't you gonna take me in?

JETHRO   Look, Fred, you don't need nobody to take you in. Just obey the white folks—do whatever they tell you, and you'll be all right.

[JETHRO *exits, after a beat.* FRED *turns and takes a few tentative steps toward the house.*]

FRED   Here in Baltimore I saw what I had never seen before: it was a white face, beaming with the most kindly emotions—the face of my new mistress, Sophia Auld.

[WHITE WOMAN *enters during above. She sits at the*

16

table, picks up the Bible, and begins to read.]

WHITE BOY   [*Enters from house and runs to* WHITE WOMAN.]
Mother! Button up my shirt!

WHITE WOMAN   I declare, little Thomas, surely the least
you can do is button your own shirt.

WHITE BOY   I want you to button it!

[WHITE WOMAN *reluctantly puts her Bible aside and
buttons his shirt. Then she looks down.*]

WHITE WOMAN   And your shoes, Thomas, you haven't even
tied your shoes—

WHITE BOY   I want you to tie them!

[*Exasperated, she starts to reach down, but catches
sight of* FRED, *who has crossed to the back yard and
is standing nearby.*]

WHITE WOMAN   Fred?

FRED   Yes, Miz Sophia.

WHITE WOMAN   [*Relieved*] Thank God, you've come at last.
Thomas, this is Fred, your slave—your uncle sent
him to stay with us and to be your body servant—

WHITE BOY   [*Excited by the prospect*] Is he really my slave?

WHITE WOMAN   Yes.

WHITE BOY   All mine, and nobody else's?

WHITE WOMAN   Yes—until your uncle takes him back.

WHITE BOY   Good! Come, Fred—

[WHITE BOY *signals* FRED *and starts off*.]

WHITE WOMAN   Wait a minute, Thomas, where are you going?

WHITE BOY   To the dockyards, to show off my new slave. Come on, Fred—

WHITE WOMAN   No, Thomas.

WHITE BOY   We'll be right back.

WHITE WOMAN   I said no. Your father will be home in a minute, and you haven't read your Bible for today.

WHITE BOY   [*Angry*] I don't want to read the Bible for today. I want to show off my slave—

WHITE WOMAN   [*Firmly*] There'll be plenty of time for that later. Now we read from the Bible.

[WHITE WOMAN *picks up the Bible, finds the place, and hands it to* WHITE BOY.]

WHITE BOY   [*Takes the book and pretends to try, then gives up*.] I don't want to—

WHITE WOMAN   Come on, Thomas, show Freddie how well you can read.

WHITE BOY   [*Shouting*] I don't want to!

[*He flings the book down and runs into the house.*]

WHITE WOMAN   Thomas! Thomas, honey, Mother didn't mean to hurt your feelings—

[*She hurries off after him.* FRED *stands a minute; then, his curiosity getting the better of him, he picks up the Bible, opens it, trying to understand what is meant by reading.* WHITE WOMAN *re-enters, carrying a pair of sandals.* FRED *is so occupied he does not see her. She approaches and looks over his shoulder.*]

WHITE WOMAN   Fred—

FRED   [*Startled, putting the book down like a hot potato*] Yes, ma'am—[*He stands before her, guilty, his head bowed, his eyes cast down in a manner he has been taught is proper for a slave.*]

WHITE WOMAN   [*Chiding, but kindly*] No, no, Fred, you mustn't bow your head to me like that. We are all of us still God's children—nor slave nor master makes a difference to Him. It says so in the Bible—this book right here that you had in your hand.

[FRED, *remembering his guilt, casts his eyes down again.*]

FRED   I'm sorry, ma'am, I didn't mean to touch it, but—

WHITE WOMAN   Fred—

FRED   [*Still not looking up*] Yes, ma'am—

WHITE WOMAN   Here are some sandals for you to wear.

[FRED *cannot manage to speak.*]

Take them.

[*He takes them.*]

Put them on, they're yours.

[FRED *tries to put the sandals on but is too nervous.*]

Would you like for me to help you?

[*She kneels and puts the sandals on* FRED, *who is stunned at such kind and gentle behavior from a white person.*]

There you are—

[FRED *stands before her, dumb, his eyes cast down, unable to say a word.*]

[*Kindly, with complete understanding*] Don't you know how to say thank you?

FRED   [*Not daring to look up at her, he finally manages it.*] Thank you, ma'am.

WHITE WOMAN   [*Suddenly occurring to her*] My lands, child, you must be starved. Have some bread and butter.

[*She turns to the table and offers it to him.* FRED *takes it but can't seem to manage to get it into his mouth.*]

WHITE WOMAN   Is something the matter?

FRED   [*Quickly*] No, ma'am—it's just that—

WHITE WOMAN   Yes?

[FRED *looks intently at the Bible. It is not difficult for her to read his thoughts.*]

Would you like for me to teach you to read?

FRED   Oh, yes, ma'am!

[*She picks up the Bible and hands it to him.* FRED *quickly puts his bread aside and picks up the Bible, getting great pleasure out of just being able to hold a book in his hands.*]

WHITE WOMAN   This is the Bible, and it is spelled B-I-B-L-E.

[FRED *looks at her in total confusion.*]

What I mean is: "Bible is a word—

[*She stops and studies him. It is obvious that he has absolutely no understanding of anything she is telling him. She sits and pulls him to her, takes the book into her own hands, and begins pointing out each letter.*]

—and every word is made up of letters, which we call the alphabet.

FRED   Alphabet.

WHITE WOMAN   Good. Now, the letter of the alphabet we use to begin the word "Bible" is called "B"—

FRED   "B"—

WHITE WOMAN   Very good, Fred, excellent. And this letter of the alphabet is called "I."

FRED   "I"—

[WHITE MAN, *as Hugh Auld, enters and stops, scarcely believing his eyes.*]

WHITE WOMAN   Now the third letter in the word "Bible" is

the same as the first letter of the word—

FRED   [*Snapping it up*] "B"!

WHITE WOMAN   [*Overjoyed at his obvious intelligence*] Excellent, Fred, excellent!

WHITE MAN   [*Shouting*] Sophia, stop!

[*He dashes over and snatches the Bible from his wife's hand.*] What are you doing?

WHITE WOMAN   I'm teaching Freddie to read—

WHITE MAN   Freddie?

WHITE WOMAN   You asked your uncle to send you a slave to be a companion to little Thomas. Freddie, this is Mr. Hugh Auld, your new master while you are in Baltimore.

[**FRED** *tries to find a proper response, but just at this moment* **WHITE BOY** *runs back on and grabs* **FRED** *by the arm and starts to pull.*]

WHITE BOY   Come on, Fred, I've got something to show you.

[**FRED** *looks to* **WHITE WOMAN**—*and* **WHITE MAN**—*for instructions.*]

Fred—I'm not ever gonna let you be my slave if you don't come on; I want to show you my new boat. Tell him, Mama—

WHITE WOMAN   [*Smiling*] It's all right, Fred.

[*A beat, then* **FRED** *and* **WHITE BOY**, *smiling at each other, run off.* **WHITE MAN** *watches them off, and then,*

to make sure he will not be overheard, he takes WHITE
WOMAN *by the arm and draws her aside.*]

WHITE MAN   What on earth are you trying to do to that boy,
ruin him?

WHITE WOMAN   Ruin him? I was only teaching him to read.

WHITE MAN   But you can't do that, Sophia!

WHITE WOMAN   Why not? He's a very bright boy.

WHITE MAN   He's a slave—and to teach a slave to read is
not only unlawful, it's unsafe, and I forbid it.

[FRED *starts back onstage in search of the bundle he
was carrying, which he has left behind, but, hearing
himself being talked about, he starts back out, then
stops in a spot where he will not be seen, and listens.*]

WHITE WOMAN   [*Deeply disturbed*] Forbid it? But Freddie
is human, and the Bible says—

WHITE MAN   Never mind what the Bible says—and for
Heaven's sakes, stop talking like an abolitionist!

WHITE WOMAN   Abolitionist?

WHITE MAN   Yes, those Yankee do-gooders, always trying
to tell us Southerners that black folks are no different
from the rest of us—can you imagine such nonsense?
Freddie is not human, not in the ways that you and
I are.

WHITE WOMAN   How can you say that of a creature that has
a soul and a mind?

WHITE MAN   But, darling, Freddie hasn't got a soul—he's black; he's a slave.

WHITE WOMAN   But all the same—

WHITE MAN   Listen to me, Sophia—reading's not only no good for a black boy like Fred; it would do him harm, make him discontent, miserable, unhappy with his lot. Now, you wouldn't want that, would you?

[WHITE WOMAN *ponders a moment.*]

WHITE WOMAN   No, but—

WHITE MAN   [*As they exit*] The worst thing in the world you can do for a slave—if you want to keep him happy—is to teach that slave to read, understand?

[*From offstage we hear a low humming, which continues under the following.*]

[*When* WHITE MAN *and* WHITE WOMAN *have gone,* FRED *comes out of hiding.*]

FRED   [*To audience*] My master's words sank deep into my heart. I now understood something that had been the greatest puzzle of all to me: the white man's power to enslave the black man. Keep the black man away from the books, keep us ignorant, and we would always be his slaves! From that moment on I understood the pathway from slavery to freedom. Come hell or high water—even if it cost me my life—I was determined to read!

[*Humming ends.*]

24

[FRED *looks around to make sure he is not being watched, then crosses to pick up the Bible, and tries to read. He walks up and down mumbling to himself, trying to make sense out of the words on the page, but without success. So deep in his preoccupation is he that he does not see that* WHITE WOMAN *has returned and stands for a moment watching. Not until he bumps into her does he lift his eyes.*]

FRED   [*Apologetic, frightened*] Oh—Miz Sophia!

WHITE WOMAN   Fred, I made a mistake—about trying to teach you to read—it's—it's not right—it's against the law.

FRED   Why is it against the law?

WHITE WOMAN   [*Snapping, trying to steel herself for what she has to do*] Don't ask me why, it just is, that's all. And if I catch you with a book, I'll have to take it away, understand?

FRED   No, ma'am.

WHITE WOMAN   You *do* understand. You are not dumb—you have a good brain in that head of yours.

FRED   But if I do have a brain, then how—

WHITE WOMAN   And, anyway, you're my property. I own you like I own a horse or a mule. You don't *need* to read, you understand?

FRED   [*Tentative, searching, earnest, really trying*] You said that all people was equal before God—that being slave or being free didn't matter before God—

WHITE WOMAN   I am not talking about God! And anyway, what God said—about people being equal—doesn't apply to you.

FRED   Why don't it, Miz Sophia?

WHITE WOMAN   [*Growing more testy*] Because you ain't people, that's why—

FRED   But, ma'am, if I ain't people—what am I?

WHITE WOMAN   You are—some kind of animal that—that looks like people but you're not!

FRED   But I can talk—and you just said I got a good brain—

WHITE WOMAN   Don't you contradict me!

FRED   And I could read, too, if—

WHITE WOMAN   [*Shouting*] You will not read! Not in my house you won't! And if I should ever catch you—

FRED   But, please, Miz Sophia—

WHITE WOMAN   Shut your sassy, impudent mouth and get out of here! Get out of here!

[WHITE WOMAN *is disturbed by what she has just done. Clutching the Bible, she hurries off.*]

[*Humming begins offstage.*]

FRED   [*To audience*] Master Hugh wasted no time. With Miz Sophia's sudden change, I began to see that slavery was harmful to the slaveowner as well as the slave. As the months passed, if I was in a separate room for any length of time, she would search me out, sure that I had found a book—but by now it was too late. The first step had already been taken: Mistress Sophia, by teaching me what little she had, had set my feet on the highway to freedom, and I wasn't going to let her—or anybody else—turn me around.

[*Humming ends.*]

[WHITE BOY *enters, this time as a schoolboy. He is barefoot, his clothes are patched and ragged; he is obviously much worse off than* FRED. FRED *watches as* WHITE BOY *passes, drawn like a magnet by the schoolbooks he carries under his arms.* FRED *suddenly has an idea, and as* WHITE BOY *passes, he snatches up the remainder of the bread and butter on the table and runs after him.*]

FRED   Hey! Hey, boy!

[WHITE BOY *does not notice him.*]

Hey, boy, wait—

[*Still no reaction*]

Hey, white boy!

WHITE BOY   You calling me?

FRED   Yeah, I'm calling you—what's your name?

WHITE BOY   My name's Robert. What's yours?

FRED   My name's Fred. I'm a slave.

WHITE BOY   I know that—well, I gotta go.

[*He starts off, but* FRED *overtakes him.*]

FRED   Hey, does your father own slaves?

WHITE BOY   No—

FRED   Why not?

WHITE BOY   [*Embarrassed*] We're too poor. We don't even have enough to eat.

[FRED *looks at* WHITE BOY. WHITE BOY *starts off again.* FRED *conspicuously brings the bread into view.*]

FRED   Hey, you hungry?

[WHITE BOY *stops, thinks a moment, then turns just in time to see* FRED *shove a big chunk of bread into his mouth.* WHITE BOY *says nothing.* FRED, *seeing the fish is hooked, chews lustily.*]

FRED   Man, this is the best bread I ever tasted.

[FRED *breaks off a piece and holds it out.*]

Want a piece?

[WHITE BOY *hesitates a moment, then crosses over to* FRED. *He reaches for the bread, but* FRED *pulls it back.*]

First, you got to answer me a question—you go to school?

WHITE BOY   [*Eyes fastened hypnotically on the bread*] Yes.

FRED   That means you know how to read, right?

WHITE BOY   Yes—

FRED   Good.

[FRED *hands* WHITE BOY *the remainder of the bread.*
WHITE BOY *puts his books down, the better to deal
with the bread, which he snatches and wolfs down
hungrily.* FRED, *with equal hunger, snatches up the
book and tries to read. When* WHITE BOY *is finished,
he wipes his mouth and reaches for his book.*]

WHITE BOY   Can I have my book now?

FRED   Sure, as soon as you teach me how to read.

WHITE BOY   It's against the law to teach you to read. You
are a slave.

FRED   Are you a slave?

WHITE BOY   Of course I'm not a slave—I'm white—

FRED   You are white, and you will be free all your life—but
I am black—

WHITE BOY   [*Thinking about it*]—which means that you
will be a slave all your life.

FRED   [*Vehemently*] I don't think that's right, do you?

WHITE BOY   [*Pondering for a moment*] No!

FRED   Then teach me to read—

WHITE BOY   What?

FRED   Master Auld say, teach a slave to read and he won't be a slave no more.

WHITE BOY   He did?

FRED   Yes—so as soon as I learn to read I'll be free, just like you. Teach me, Robert—teach me to read from your book—will you?

[WHITE BOY *begins to respond to* FRED's *enthusiasm.*]

WHITE BOY   [*Excited*] Of course I will.

[*They take the book between them as they sit down on the floor—then they begin.*]

WHITE BOY   First, the alphabet—"A"—

FRED   "A"—

WHITE BOY   "B"—

FRED   "B"—

WHITE BOY   "C"—

FRED   "C"—

WHITE BOY   "D"—

FRED   "D"—

[*So caught up are they in the lesson that they do not see that* WHITE WOMAN *has entered and is spying on them.*]

WHITE BOY   "E"—

FRED   "E"—

WHITE BOY   "F"—

FRED   "F"—

[WHITE WOMAN *sneaks up behind the two boys on the floor.*]

WHITE BOY   "G"—

FRED   "G"—

WHITE BOY   "H"—

[WHITE WOMAN *snatches the book from* WHITE BOY'S *fingers.* FRED *and* WHITE BOY *jump up.*]

WHITE WOMAN   Caught you!

[*She tears the book up and flings the pieces to the ground.*]

WHITE BOY   Please, ma'am, we was only—

WHITE WOMAN   I know what you were doing—ruining a perfectly good slave! Now get out of here!

[*She hands broom to* FRED.]

And you get to your work!

[*She chases* WHITE BOY *offstage.*]

FRED   [*Crosses to pick up the torn pages of the book.*] From this time on she watched me like a hawk—because everything I could find with print on it I tried to read, even if I couldn't understand it all the time.

[FRED *opens the book and begins to read.*]

31

Escape to Freedom

[*Offstage we hear voices singing "Lord I Don't Feel No Ways Tired."*]

COMPANY

I am seeking for a city
Hallelujah
I am seeking for a city
Hallelujah
For a city into the heaven
Hallelujah
For a city into the heaven
Hallelujah

CHILDREN

Lord I don't (I don't) feel no ways tired

COMPANY

Oh glory hallelujah
For I hope to shout glory when this world is on fire

CHILDREN

Oh glory hallelujah

[*During the song* FRED, *subconsciously responding to the beat of the music, moves across the stage, reading with one eye and keeping watch with the other. He exits and immediately re-enters, this time carrying a newspaper.*]

[*The cast continues humming the melody of the song from offstage as* FRED *continues.*]

FRED   [*Reading aloud*] The general sentiment of mankind is that a man who will not fight for himself, when he has the means to do so, is not worth—

[*He throws newspaper to the ground in frustration.*]

[*The humming ends abruptly.*]

FRED   [*To audience*] As I read, I began to realize how much had been denied me as a slave. But my reading didn't show me the way to escape. I finally felt that learning to read had been not a blessing but a curse. Like Master said—the more I read, the more miserable I became.

[WHITE BOY *and* WHITE WOMAN *enter, laughing, hugging, and kissing each other. He is dressed as a sailor and she as a loose and gaudy woman of the town. They continue fondling and laughing; neither is aware that* FRED, *made somewhat bold by his anger, is watching them.*]

WHITE WOMAN   [*Finally pulling free*] I've got to go now.

WHITE BOY   I'll go with you.

WHITE WOMAN   No, you wait here, till I come back.

[*She starts off, but* WHITE BOY *pulls her back.*]

WHITE BOY   How about a little something to last me till you return?

[*She laughs as he pulls her to him.*]

WHITE WOMAN   You Yankee sailors are all devils, aren't you?

WHITE BOY   Sure are!

[*He grabs her, spins her around, and they kiss.*

Suddenly she spots FRED *and pulls free again.*]

WHITE WOMAN   What you looking at, boy?

[FRED *is still a slave, but manages, out of his anger, to stand his ground.*]

I'm talking to you, nigger!

WHITE BOY   Aw, let the fellow alone.

WHITE WOMAN   He's a slave.

WHITE BOY   So what—he's still human.

WHITE WOMAN   He's a slave, and he's got no business spying on people in a public place. He ought to be whipped!

WHITE BOY   Aw, honey, you can't mean that—he's only a kid!

WHITE WOMAN   I do mean it. I don't know how you all treat 'em up North, but down here in Maryland—

WHITE BOY   All right, all right, you run right along and I'll take care of it.

WHITE WOMAN   Ought to be whipped, that's what!

WHITE BOY   I'll take care of it—you run on along—

[*She starts offstage.*]

—and hurry back!

[WHITE WOMAN *exits. The sailor, obviously a good-natured man, chuckles as he crosses to* FRED, *who, though frightened, is determined, for the first time, to stand his ground.*]

34

WHITE BOY   You're the first person I ever met who was a
slave.

FRED   Yeah, but that don't make me no different from you
or her or anybody else.

WHITE BOY   [*Laughing*] I didn't say it did.

FRED   I got brains just like you got brains, and I can think
just as good as you can think, and I can read just as
good as you can read!

WHITE BOY   [*Trying to explain it, but not knowing how*]
Look, son, I know how you feel.

FRED   How can you know how I feel? You're not black.

WHITE BOY   No, I'm not black, and I'm not a slave—but if I
were, I'd do something about it.

FRED   [*His curiosity overcoming his feelings*] Do what?

WHITE BOY   I'd run away first chance I got.

FRED   [*Suspicious*] Why should I run away?

WHITE BOY   [*Matter-of-factly*] Why stay?

[FRED, *not sure that this is not a trap, refuses to answer directly.*]

FRED   I knew a slave who ran away once—but they caught
him and beat him and sold him down the river.

WHITE BOY   They might catch you—that's a chance you'll
have to take—but if you don't take the chance, you'll
never be free, right?

35

FRED   But where could I go?

WHITE BOY   You could go up north—there are people up north doing all they can to end slavery.

FRED   What people?

WHITE BOY   Abolitionists—white people and black people, who hate slavery as much as you do. They'd hide you, feed you, give you clothes and money. As a matter of fact, I heard about a young fellow who dressed himself in a sailor suit, like mine, and wrote himself a pass.

FRED   A pass? What's that?

WHITE BOY   A pass is a little slip of paper a master gives to a slave when he sends him on an errand by himself.

FRED   This slave you're talking about—he wrote out his own pass, you say?

WHITE BOY   Yes, he signed his master's name to it and then went down to the boat, and got right on, big as you please. Anybody asked him what he was doing, he'd show them his pass, written in his own hand, and tell them he was traveling on business for his master.

FRED   And he got away?

WHITE BOY   All the way to New York. And if he did it, so can you. Look—as a matter of fact—

[*He reaches into his pocket and brings out a piece of paper and a pencil.*]—I'll show you how. Here, take this and write down what I tell you.

[FRED *seats himself on a convenient object, takes the* *paper and pencil, and holds them in readiness.*]

"This pass will certify that—"

[FRED *starts to write but stops.*]

What's the matter?

FRED   [*Just discovering this fact himself*] I can't write.

WHITE BOY   Can't write? But I thought you said—

FRED   I said I could read--I taught myself how to read— but not to write.

WHITE BOY   Oh, I see.

[*Pauses a moment, then makes a decision.*]

All right, I'll teach you to write.

[*He takes pencil and paper from* FRED *and proceeds to demonstrate. Writing*] This—pass—will—certify —that—[*To* FRED] What did you say your name was?

FRED   My name is Frederick.

[*Looks up and sees* WHITE WOMAN, *who has returned and is watching.*]

WHITE WOMAN   [*Suspicious—to sailor*] What are you doing?

WHITE BOY   I was just teaching young Frederick to—

FRED   [*Rising in agitation*] No, he wasn't! He wasn't doing no such a thing!

WHITE WOMAN Down here it's against the law to teach slaves to read and write.

WHITE BOY [*Laughing*] Who's teaching anybody anything?

[*He rises, looking at her.*]

My, but don't you look wonderful!

[*He holds the paper and pencil behind his back and gestures for* FRED *to take them from him.*]

WHITE WOMAN [*Eating it up*] I do? I went all the way back home just to get these earrings; I do hope you like them—

WHITE BOY Like them? Hon, I love them!

[*Takes her by the arm and starts off.*]

Just wait till I get you downtown so the rest of the boys can see you!

[*He manages to get the pencil and paper back to* FRED *without her noticing, and then they exit.* FRED *watches after them a moment, then turns in high excitement to resume his story.*]

FRED [*To audience*] There was no better place in all Baltimore to start the second part of my education than right where I was—in the shipyard.

[*We hear the cast humming "Lord I Don't Feel No Ways Tired" as they change the set to an arrangement suggesting a shipyard, with coils of rope, planks, etc.,* strewn about the stage. This continues under the following.]

I remember seeing ship's carpenters at the dock cut pieces of timber into planks—

[FRED crosses to a plank, picks it up and examines it.]

They would write on the plank with a piece of chalk the part of the ship for which it was intended.

[FRED holds the plank in such a way that we can clearly see the letter "L" that has been handwritten upon it.]

"L," that's for larboard.

[FRED takes a piece of chalk and laboriously writes several imitations of the "L," using an appropriate spot on the pier, or on the board, as a blackboard. When he is satisfied, he sets the plank down and picks up another.]

"S," for starboard.

[FRED repeats the previous action during the following, putting one plank down as soon as he is finished, and picking up another.]

"L.F.," that's for larboard forward; "S.A.," that's for starboard aft. In a short while I could do "L," "S," "F," and "A" with no trouble at all.

[He indicates his mastery with a flourish.]

And not only planks—during this time any board

wall or brick fence or pavement that had any writing on it became my copybook.

[FRED *moves quickly from one appropriate place, construction, or object to another, copying the indicated lettering. In his movings about, he finds a half-torn book.*]

I found a Webster Spelling Book that had written script in it.

[FRED *busily copies from the book, making the lettering on every nearby object.* WHITE BOY *and* WHITE WOMAN, *as children, enter, skipping, and hand their copybooks to* FRED.]

When my little white friends finished with their lettering books at school, they gave them to me.

[FRED *takes the books, thanks* WHITE BOY *and* WHITE WOMAN, *who exit, and then* FRED *goes busily to work.*]

I copied—and copied—and copied—until I had mastered every letter of the alphabet. "Z"!

[FRED *writes a final "Z" on some appropriate surface, then stands back, in pride and satisfaction, to admire his handiwork: every place he looks, everything he sees, has some evidence of* FRED's *capacity to write.*]

I was now ready to try my hand at the most important thing of all: writing a pass.

COMPANY   [*Offstage*]
Lord I don't (I don't) feel no ways tired

CHILDREN

Oh glory hallelujah

COMPANY

For I hope to shout glory when this world is on fire

CHILDREN

Oh glory hallelujah

FRED [*Takes out pencil and paper, reading as he writes.*] This—is—to—certify—that I—the undersigned— have given the bearer, my servant, Fred Bailey, full liberty to go to—

[FRED *looks up and sees* BLACK MAN, *as* JETHRO, *standing over him.*]

Hey, Jethro, look what I just did—

[*Something about* JETHRO's *face makes him stop.*]

JETHRO [*Sadly*] Ol' Master's dead, Fred.

FRED Dead? Colonel Lloyd?

JETHRO Yes, so all the slaves is being called back to the plantation so the property can be divided up.

FRED Jethro, I can't go back—with this pass I can get to—

JETHRO What?

FRED Never mind.

JETHRO I was sent to get you, and if you don't come, I'm in trouble, and you, too. Come on, Fred.

[JETHRO *exits.* FRED *starts to exit with him, but turns back to the audience.*]

Scene Three

[*During the following, the cast moves the set to an arrangement suggesting a rough country farm.* FRED's *demeanor is different—it is obvious that he is now involved in hard work for the first time in his entire life—work for which he is entirely unsuited.*]

FRED [*To audience*] The whole dream of my life had been to escape from slavery. Yet here I was at seventeen years of age, still a slave, back at St. Michael's on a farm, being forced to do things I had never done before: what good would my reading and writing do me now? In Baltimore with Master Hugh I had at least been fed well enough and given shoes and decent clothes—and there was always the chance that somehow I might escape! But not here at St. Michael's—Master Thomas and his wife, Rowena, not only watched me like a hawk, night and day, but also they were the meanest and stingiest people I ever saw in my life.

[WHITE MAN *enters, as Thomas Auld, dressed for church, moving across the stage. He speaks as he moves.*]

WHITE MAN   Don't just stand there gawking, boy, go hitch the horse and buggy.

FRED   Yes, sir, but first could we maybe have a little breakfast?

WHITE MAN   [*Stops and turns to* FRED.] So, looks like you've been in Baltimore too long, boy—my brother, Hugh, and that fancy wife of his have near-about ruined you, I suspect—just look at him, all fat and sassy— dressed up good as any white man—I bet you think you are as good as a white man, don't you, boy? And drop your eyes when I'm talking to you!

[FRED *does so.*]

That's better.

[WHITE MAN *turns and exits.*]

FRED   [*To audience*] And his wife, Rowena—

[WHITE WOMAN, *as Rowena Auld, enters, also dressed for church, and moves rapidly across in opposite direction.*]

WHITE WOMAN   This ain't Baltimore, boy—you heard Mr.

43

Thomas—get the horse and buggy. We're late already!

FRED   [*Tries to stop her*] Yes, ma'am, but we ain't had nothing to eat!

[*She exits.* FRED *shouts after her.*]

You expect us black folks to work around this damned old farm like dogs and you won't even feed us!

[*He turns to face the audience again, and as he speaks the stage is being changed to suggest the interior of a church.*]

It was bad: if we slaves hadn't learned to *steal* in order to feed and to clothe ourselves, we might have died from hunger and exposure.

[*The* COMPANY *has assembled on stage as if they were in church.* WHITE BOY, *dressed as a minister, Cookman, holds a Bible in his hand.* WHITE MAN *and* WHITE WOMAN *are his white audience, standing in the front row. Behind them are the slaves:* BLACK MAN, BLACK WOMAN, *and* BLACK BOY, *who are looking on with interest. They are humming "Give Me That Old-Time Religion."*]

FRED   But one night my master and his wife went to a revival meeting. And something totally unexpected happened.

[FRED *moves to join the slaves in the back row as the song begins.*]

44

COMPANY

> *Give me that old-time religion*
> *Give me that old-time religion*
> *Give me that old-time religion*
> *It's good enough for me*
>
> *Give me that old-time religion*
> *Give me that old-time religion*
> *Give me that old-time religion*
> *It's good enough for me*

BLACK WOMAN

> *It was good for my old mother*
> *It was good for my old mother*
> *It was good for my old mother*
> *It's good enough for me*

COMPANY

> *Give me that old-time religion*
> *Give me that old-time religion*
> *Give me that old-time religion*
> *It's good enough for me*

BLACK WOMAN

> *It was good enough for master*
> *It was good enough for master*
> *It was good enough for master*
> *It's good enough for me*

[*During the song* WHITE MAN *has been trembling; now he jumps as if suddenly struck by lightning. He dances, shouts, groans, and falls writhing to the floor in the complete ecstasy of religious conversion.*]

WHITE MAN   Oh Lord, I'm saved!

WHITE BOY   Hallelujah!

WHITE MAN   I've been redeemed!

WHITE BOY   Oh, glory!

WHITE MAN   I love everybody!

[WHITE BOY *and the rest respond with fervor: "Amen!"* *"Hallelujah!" "Oh, give praises!"*]

Everybody is my brother!

[WHITE MAN *runs around the stage in his frenzy,* *grabbing, hugging, shaking hands with black and* *white. Even* FRED *responds to this, his hope being—* *as is that of all the slaves—that the master's conver-* *sion will make life better.*]

Everybody is my sister! I love everybody! There is peace in my heart! There is joy in my soul! I love everybody! I love everybody!

[WHITE WOMAN *and* WHITE BOY *help* WHITE MAN *off-* *stage.* FRED *follows them with his eyes, then turns* *again to the audience, while the* COMPANY *rearranges* *the set to suggest a Sunday-school classroom.*]

FRED   Could it be true? Could it be that my master had really changed? Had he really come to believe that everybody—including black slaves like me—were really his brothers and sisters?

[*To* WHITE BOY, *who has entered with an armload of* *books and papers*] Do you believe it, Mr. Cookman?

Do you believe Master Thomas has really changed?

WHITE BOY   God moves in mysterious ways—his wonders to perform. Here, help me with these.

[FRED *takes some of the books and papers from his arms and helps distribute them to the slaves, who are sitting on the benches waiting for the lesson to begin.*]

FRED   You really think Master Thomas is going to allow us to hold Sunday school for the rest of the slaves?

WHITE BOY   Frederick—where is your faith?

FRED   [*To audience*] Mr. Cookman was a fine man, a member of our church who hated slavery as much as I did, and he and I had decided to set up a Sunday school in a house nearby.

[FRED *crosses in to scene.*]

WHITE BOY   [*To the class*] Though you are slaves and I am not, in God's sight all men are equal, all men are brothers.

[BLACK WOMAN *stands to ask a question.*]

BLACK WOMAN   Is Master Thomas equal too?

WHITE BOY   Master Thomas is a Christian; he has accepted Christ, and that means—

[BLACK MAN *rises.*]

BLACK MAN   That means all mens, and all womens, are Master Thomas's brothers and sisters—no matter they black or white—ain't that right, Fred?

FRED [*Skeptical*] We'll see. We'll see. Now, the purpose of this Sunday school is to teach you—all of you—to read and write.

[BLACK WOMAN *rises.*]

BLACK WOMAN Do reading and writing make people free?

[FRED *and* WHITE BOY *look at each other.*]

WHITE BOY No, I'm afraid not, but—

FRED —but it can help. For instance, there was a slave in Baltimore who learned to read and write, and the first thing he did was to write himself a pass—

BLACK WOMAN A pass?

FRED A pass is a piece of paper, like this—

[*Shows slave's pass.*]

—with writing on it—like this—that says: this black man, or this black woman, is free.

[*He looks at each of them intently.*]

BLACK MAN You mean—if I had a paper like that—I'd be free?

FRED Well, down here in Maryland where everybody knows that you and me belong to Master Thomas, no. But if you were to run away and go up north to Pennsylvania or to New York—

BLACK WOMAN You can read, Fred, and you can write?

FRED Yes, I can.

BLACK WOMAN   Well, in that case, why ain't *you* run away? Why ain't *you* free?

[FRED *and* WHITE BOY *look at each other.*]

WHITE BOY   [*Quickly*] Let us bow our heads in prayer. Oh, Lord, we ask thy blessings on this our Sunday school and on all of us thy children and equal in thy sight, and on our newly converted brother Master Thomas Auld. Help him to see, oh, Lord, that in thy sight that none are slaves, that all, indeed, are free, that all of us regardless of the color of our skin are indeed sisters and brothers—

[WHITE MAN, *carrying a whip, and* WHITE WOMAN, *brandishing a broom, come running in, shouting.*]

WHITE MAN *and* WHITE WOMAN   Caught you, caught you, caught you!

[WHITE MAN *starts beating the slaves with his whip.* WHITE WOMAN *takes after* FRED *with her broom.*]

WHITE MAN   Teach slaves to read and write, will you? Over my dead body!

[FRED *and the other slaves are driven off.* WHITE MAN *picks up a fallen book and waves it in the face of* WHITE BOY.]

WHITE BOY.   But you're converted, Master Thomas, you're a Christian!

WHITE MAN   Get off my property! Before I take my gun and blow you off! And take your filthy junk with you!

[WHITE BOY *quickly gathers up whatever books and papers have fallen, and exits.*]

Dirty abolitionist—

WHITE WOMAN   You *know* who's behind all this, don't you? You know who started it?

WHITE MAN   Frederick?

WHITE WOMAN   Frederick! Reading, writing, all them books —I warned you.

WHITE MAN   But I took his books. I threw them away.

WHITE WOMAN   Don't do no good, taking 'em—he always seems to find some more somewhere—

WHITE MAN   And now he's teaching the *others* to read and write—that's what makes him so dangerous. What are we to do with that boy, Rowena?

[*They both ponder a moment; then* WHITE WOMAN *has an idea.*]

WHITE WOMAN   Well, there is one thing we can do: we can send him to Covey's.

WHITE MAN   Send him to Covey's—why didn't I think of that?

WHITE WOMAN   Covey will break him—

WHITE MAN   Of course—we'll send that arrogant, bullheaded boy to Covey's!

[*They exit smiling.*]

Scene Four

[*During the song the* COMPANY *changes the set to Covey's slave-breaking plantation as they sing.*]

COMPANY

> *Look a-yonder (huh)*
> *Hot boiling sun coming over (huh)*
> *Look a-yonder*
> *Hot boiling sun coming over (huh)*
> *And it ain't going down*
> *And it ain't going down*
>
> *Thought you wasn't coming (huh)*
> *Thought you wasn't coming this morning (huh)*
> *Thought you wasn't coming*
> *Thought you wasn't coming this morning (huh)*
> *But you're here on time*
> *But you're here on time*

[FRED *is standing waiting.* WHITE MAN, *as Covey, stands reading a letter which* FRED *has given him.*]

FRED   [*To audience*] Covey was a slave breaker—if a slave was rebellious and stubborn and did not obey orders quickly enough, he was sent to Covey's for a period of one year to be tamed.

[WHITE MAN *folds the note, puts it into his pocket, and crosses to look* FRED *over.*]

WHITE MAN   So—they tell me you can read and write like a white man.

FRED   Yessir—

WHITE MAN   Well, first time I catch you with a book or a pencil and paper, I'll break your neck, is that clear?

FRED   Yessir—

WHITE MAN   Speak up, boy, I can't hear you!

FRED   [*Louder*] Yessir.

WHITE MAN   And don't look at me—look down on the ground like you're supposed to.

[*He slaps the ground with his whip.* FRED *does not answer, but lowers his eyes as ordered.*]

Now, the first thing I want you to do is to go yonder where them two oxen is and hitch them up.

[FRED *looks off.*]

Go, boy, and bring them here and be quick about it.

[WHITE MAN *stands and watches as* FRED *returns with* WHITE BOY *and* BLACK BOY, *who are costumed in a manner suggesting that they are the two oxen.*]

FRED   [*Totally at sea*] What do I do now, sir?

WHITE MAN   Listen carefully—I don't intend to tell you this more than once. This is the in-hand ox. His name is Buck. And this is the off-hand ox. Call him Darby. You understand?

FRED   [*Trying to get it straight.*] In-hand ox, Buck—off-hand ox, Darby—yessir—

WHITE MAN   Want them to start, say Giddap.

FRED   Giddap!

WHITE MAN   Want them to stop, say Whoa!

FRED   Say Whoa, yessir.

WHITE MAN   For turning to the right it's Gee! For turning to the left it's Haw! Got that?

FRED   To the right is Gee, to the left is Haw. Whoa!

[*The oxen turn to the right, to the left, and stop.*]

WHITE MAN   Now get on down to the thicket and bring me back a cartload of firewood.

FRED   [*Anxious to please*] A cartload of firewood—

WHITE MAN   And if you're not back in an hour I'm coming after you with my whip. Now get going!

FRED   Get going, yessir.

[FRED *fiddles with the reins as he gives himself a quick refresher.*]

In-ox—off-ox—Gee is for right—Haw is for left—Giddap, oxen!

[*The oxen start off.*]

Go right, oxen, go right—I mean Gee! Gee!

[*The oxen go right.*]

Haw, oxen, Haw!

[FRED *has to pull hard on the reins, but the oxen finally go left.*]

Straighten up now, oxen, I mean—go forward—I mean Giddap. No, not Giddap, I mean Whoa, oxen, Whoa!

[*But the oxen pay no attention as they pull the protesting* FRED *along.* WHITE MAN *stands and watches him with a wicked smile. The oxen move across the stage, gathering speed as they travel, until finally they drag the cart through a gate and knock it down.* FRED *falls to the ground and, before he can rise,* WHITE MAN *is on him with the whip.*]

WHITE MAN   Break down my gate, will you, you lazy, trifling thing—tear up my property—I'll fix you!

[FRED *staggers to his feet, but the blows are coming so fast and furious he can barely manage to keep on his feet as he stumbles offstage,* WHITE MAN *right behind him, still laying it on.*]

[BLACK MAN, BLACK WOMAN, BLACK BOY, *and* FRED *enter, humming a low noise, and all lie in a heap at center, as if asleep. From offstage we hear a blast from the driver's horn, jolting them awake.* WHITE MAN *leaps onstage yelling, stomping, and cracking his whip—a new workday has begun.*]

WHITE MAN [*At the top of his voice*] Rise up—rise up, I tell you, rise up! Let's everybody rise up and hit that cornfield! Rise up, I say!

[*The* SLAVES *rise up, stiff and stumbling, moving slowly at first, bumping into each other. Not yet fully awake, trying, as they grope about, to escape the ever-present lash.* WHITE BOY *stands by, with rifle, to make sure they do as they are told. The* SLAVES *sing:*]

SLAVES

     Look a-yonder (*huh*)
     Hot boiling sun coming over (*huh*)
     Look a-yonder
     Hot boiling sun coming over (*huh*)
     And it ain't going down
     And it ain't going down

[*A trough of porridge is pulled in from offstage by* WHITE WOMAN, *as Covey's wife, and the* SLAVES *dip their hands into the porridge and stuff their mouths as quickly as they can, before she drags it off. As ever,* WHITE MAN *circles around and among them, pushing, shouting, making sure that everybody keeps moving.*]

     No I don't
     No I don't

> *No I don't, don't, don't*
> *No I don't*
> *I don't like no redneck boss man*
> *No I don't*
>
> *Had to get up this morning too soon*
> *Had to get up this morning too soon*
> *Had to get up this morning too soon, soon*
> *Had to get up this morning too soon*

[*Quickly the slaves fall in line and start running in place, pantomiming running to the cornfield.* WHITE MAN *cracks his whip as he pantomimes riding a horse alongside them.*]

> *You better run, run, run, run, run, run*
> *You better run, run, run, run, run, run*
> *You better run to the city of refuge*

[*The song speeds up as the* SLAVES *run faster and faster. All the time,* WHITE MAN *ad-libs "Move it!" etc.*]

> *You better run, run, run, run, run, run*
> *You better run, run, run, run, run, run*
> *You better run, run, run, run, run, run*
> *You better run to the city of refuge*

WHITE MAN   All right, hit that cornfield!

[*The* SLAVES *slow down and finally stop, already exhausted. They mime picking corn as they sing:*]

SLAVES

> *No I don't*
> *No I don't*

No I don't, don't, don't
No I don't
I don't like no redneck boss man
No I don't

Had to get up this morning in such a haste
Didn't have time to wash my face
Had to get up this morning too soon
Had to get up this morning too soon
Had to get up this morning too soon, soon
Had to get up this morning too soon

No I don't
No I don't
No I don't, don't, don't
No I don't
I don't like no redneck boss man
No I don't

WHITE MAN   Quitting time!

[*The* SLAVES *fall down, exhausted.* FRED *spills a sack of corn.* WHITE MAN *is infuriated.*]

WHITE MAN   You lazy thing! Spill my corn, will you!

[FRED *falls to the ground;* WHITE MAN *exits.*]

[*From offstage we hear* WHITE BOY *and* WHITE WOMAN *singing "Go Tell It on the Mountain." The song continues under the dialogue.*]

WHITE BOY *and* WHITE WOMAN
            Go tell it on the mountain
            Over the hills and everywhere

> *Go tell it on the mountain*
> *That Jesus Christ is born*
>
> *Go tell it on the mountain*
> *Over the hills and everywhere*
> *Go tell it on the mountain*
> *That Jesus Christ is born*

WHITE BOY

> *He made me a watchman*
> *Upon the city wall*
> *And if I am a Christian*
> *I am the least of all*

WHITE BOY *and* WHITE WOMAN

> *Go tell it on the mountain*
> *Over the hills and everywhere*
> *Go tell it on the mountain*
> *That Jesus Christ is born*

WHITE MAN

All right, all right, all right, all right, all of you come
on out here!

[BLACK MAN, BLACK WOMAN, BLACK BOY, *and* FRED *all
drag themselves in and stand, bone weary, before*
WHITE MAN. WHITE BOY *and* WHITE WOMAN *enter with
presents for the* SLAVES.]

WHITE MAN

Today is Christmas, birthday of our Lord and Savior,
Jesus Christ. It's a holiday—for everybody—and that
means no more work until tomorrow.

[*The* SLAVES *begin to perk up at the news.* WHITE BOY

and WHITE WOMAN *distribute presents to the* SLAVES.]

Remember—Christ our Savior was born on this day, and that's good news not only to us white folks, but also to you niggers. And I can swear to you that if you all work hard, behave yourselves, and don't give me and your masters no trouble, there's gonna be a place for you—a special place for all good niggers—right up there in Heaven!

[*He picks up a gallon brown jug.*]

So eat, sing, dance—all you want—and here's a jug of corn spirits for all of you. Drink up, everybody! Drink up, I say!

[*He hands the jug to* BLACK MAN, *who drinks from it and passes it on to the other* SLAVES.]

Let's liven this thing up for Heaven's sake. I want to hear me some singing and I want to see me some dancing—and I mean right now!

[WHITE MAN *begins to pat his foot and clap his hands, singing "Blue-Tail Fly" as he does so. The* SLAVES *join in as they continue drinking, singing, strutting, giggling, laughing, staggering, playfully tussling among themselves for another drink from the brown jug, much to the delight of the whites, who laugh and are highly amused.* FRED *stands on watching in undisguised disgust.*]

SLAVES

> *Jimmy crack corn and I don't care*
> *Jimmy crack corn and I don't care*

Jimmy crack corn and I don't care
The master's gone away

When I was young I used to wait
Upon old master and pass the plate
And fetch the bottle when he got dry
And brush away the blue-tail fly

Jimmy crack corn and I don't care
Jimmy crack corn and I don't care
Jimmy crack corn and I don't care
The master's gone away

WHITE WOMAN [*Moving in to break it up*] All right, all right, it's time. Come on, everybody, let's go up to the big house. I got some friends up there who are just dying to see you darkies sing and dance. Come on, come on!

[*Everyone except* FRED *exits, singing another chorus of "Blue-Tail Fly."* FRED *turns to the audience.*]

FRED Dancing, singing—and drinking whiskey. The slave masters knew that if they could just make us drunk, we would forget our misery; if they could keep us singing and dancing and cuttin' the fool like a bunch of idiots we wouldn't be angry any more—would lose our desire to fight back—to escape. "Merry Christmas" and "Happy New Year"! And for a lot of us— tired, ignorant, not knowing any better—that's exactly what it was. But not for me. Holidays on a slave plantation only made me madder, and sadder, and more miserable than I had ever been before.

[BLACK MAN, BLACK WOMAN, BLACK BOY, *and* WHITE MAN *enter. The* SLAVES *mime a wheat-threshing operation. They sing one line of "Death's Gonna Lay His Cold Icy Hands on Me" as they get into place, and then freeze.*]

SLAVES

Oh Death
Death's gonna lay his cold icy hands on me

[WHITE MAN *walks over to* FRED.]

WHITE MAN   Now, you ain't no good at all in the cornfield, so I'm gonna try you out at another job. I'm leaving you here to fan wheat—and if you don't do no better at fanning wheat than you did at picking corn, God help you!

[WHITE MAN *exits.*]

FRED   [*To audience*] In a short while Covey succeeded in breaking me—in body, soul, and spirit. My mind was a blank. All interest I had ever had in reading and writing, in any books at all, I completely lost. Covey had finally made me what I swore I would never become: a nigger and a slave. I would have been better off if I were dead.

[FRED *turns and crosses up to partake in the work of fanning wheat. As he moves into the routine, we hear a song from the* SLAVES: *"Death's Gonna Lay His Cold Icy Hands on Me." As the song proceeds, we begin to see that* FRED *is having an even tougher time trying to fan wheat than he did picking corn. The stage ac-*

tion here must suggest some operation by which a bundle of wheat is fed into a machine which threshes it, separating the wheat from the chaff. FRED *is engaged in carrying huge bundles to the machine and placing them properly, then bending down, picking up the chaff, and carrying it away. He then picks up another bundle, moves to the machine where the whole operation is repeated.* FRED *always winds up just a little behind.*]

SLAVES

Oh Death
Death's gonna lay his cold icy hands on me
Oh Death
Death's gonna lay his cold icy hands on me

Master holler hurry
Death's gonna lay his cold icy hands on me
But I'm gonna take my time
Death's gonna lay his cold icy hands on me

Oh Death
Death's gonna lay his cold icy hands on me
Oh Death
Death's gonna lay his cold icy hands on me

He say he's making money
Death's gonna lay his cold icy hands on me
But I'm making time
Death's gonna lay his cold icy hands on me

Oh Death
Death's gonna lay his cold icy hands on me

> *Oh Death*
> *Death's gonna lay his cold icy hands on me*
>
> *Oh Death*
> *Death's gonna lay his cold icy hands on me*
> *Oh Death . . .*

[FRED *has become so exhausted that he begins to stagger.* BLACK MAN *and* BLACK WOMAN *look at him with growing concern. They know he will soon collapse, but dare not stop to help him. Finally* FRED *falls under the weight of the huge bundle of wheat he is carrying. He tries to rise, gets as far as his knees, then tumbles over again—this time he just lies there.*]

BLACK MAN   Fred! Fred!

BLACK WOMAN   Oh, my Lord, Fred!

[*They run over to the prostrate boy and try to lift him.* WHITE MAN *suddenly appears.*]

WHITE MAN   [*To the slaves*] Back to your work!

BLACK WOMAN   But Freddie's sick, Mr. Covey!

WHITE MAN   Back to your work, I say, all of you!

[*The* SLAVES *go back to work, slowly.* WHITE MAN *stands over* FRED *and kicks him.*]

All right, boy, up on your feet.

[FRED *groans and tries to rise. In background* BLACK MAN, BLACK WOMAN, *and* BLACK BOY *try to operate the machine, though shorthanded, and to keep an eye on what* WHITE MAN *is doing to* FRED.]

Up on your feet, I tell you!

[WHITE MAN *reaches down and snatches* FRED *to his feet.* FRED *wobbles unsteadily, but finally is able— just barely—to stand.*]

Now get on back to work!

[FRED *wants to move but dares not, afraid that he might fall.*]

FRED   I can't, Mr. Covey—

WHITE MAN   Damn you, boy, I said get back to work!

FRED   [*Still wobbling*] I can't, Mr. Covey, I just can't! I—

WHITE MAN   [*Shouting*] This is the last time that I am going to tell you, boy—get on back to work!

[FRED *tries to move, but his trembling legs refuse to obey.*]

FRED   I can't, Mr. Covey—I can't!

[WHITE MAN *grabs up a hefty barrel stave.*]

WHITE MAN   Oh, yes, you can—I'll help you!

[*He raises the stave and advances on* FRED.]

BLACK MAN   Don't hit him, Mr. Covey, please, sir!

BLACK WOMAN   We'll make it up for him, Mr. Covey!

WHITE MAN   Shut up and get back to work, the both of you!

[BLACK MAN *and* BLACK WOMAN *return to their opera-tion.* WHITE MAN *turns to* FRED.]

I knowed the minute I set eyes on you that one day I would have to teath you who was the boss on this here plantation!

[*He hits* FRED *across the shoulders with the stave and knocks him down.*]

Tell me, boy—what do your books have to say to you now?

[FRED *staggers to his feet, and* WHITE MAN *knocks him down again.*]

What good is your reading now, eh, boy?

[FRED *staggers to his feet.* WHITE MAN *swings again, but this time* FRED *somehow manages to duck and avoid the blow.* WHITE MAN *is angered.*]

So that's your game, is it? I'll show you!

[*He swings again.* FRED *wobbles but manages to get out of the way again.* WHITE MAN, *toppled by the force of his own blow, falls heavily to the floor. Im-mediately he springs to his feet, drawing his pistol from his belt at the same time, but before he can shoot,* FRED *snatches the pistol and flings it offstage.* WHITE MAN *is now not so sure of himself, for all of a sudden the nature of the battle has changed.* FRED *is still on his feet, wobbling, but not cringing any more.* WHITE MAN *rushes, but this time* FRED *steps aside, grabs* WHITE MAN's *arm and twists it until the stave*

65

drops. WHITE MAN *leaps free and turns to face* FRED, *who kicks the stave clear. He then moves forward, crouched, to confront his attacker. From background the* SLAVES *watch with keen interest this change in circumstances.*]

WHITE MAN   [*Trying to finesse it*] All right, boy, I'm ordering you—you go on back to work.

FRED   [*Moving forward*] Make me, Mr. Covey—you make me go back to work—

WHITE MAN   [*Beginning to circle away*] I'm warning you one more time, get back to work or I'll kill you!

FRED   [*Still moving in*] That may well be, Mr. Covey, maybe you will kill me—but if you don't, I sure intend to kill you!

WHITE MAN   [*Appealing to the* SLAVES] Hey, some of you all better talk to this nigger boy—I think he's gone crazy!

FRED   I ain't crazy, Mr. Covey, and I ain't a nigger boy—not any more. I am a man—a *man*, Covey—as much of a man as you are—or more!

[*Suddenly* WHITE MAN *ducks and picks up the stave, toward which he had been inching all along. He swings it at* FRED's *head.* FRED *ducks, moves in, grabs him in a bear hug and squeezes with all his might. In the frantic struggle to free himself,* WHITE MAN *drops the stave, then* FRED *wrestles him to the ground. They twist and turn as* WHITE MAN *struggles to free himself from* FRED's *grasp. They roll around and thrash about until* FRED *finally winds up on top, his hands clutched around* WHITE MAN's *throat, squeezing.*]

WHITE MAN   [*His voice hoarse*] Sarah! Toby! Pull him off of me, pull him off!

BLACK MAN   We can't stop to pull nobody off of you, Mr. Covey!

BLACK WOMAN   You told us to keep on working, Mr. Covey, and that's just what we gonna do!

[*They keep on working, furiously. The struggle continues until* WHITE MAN *breaks* FRED's *grip and scrambles to his feet.* FRED *scrambles up, too, ready to resume the battle.* WHITE MAN *backs away.*]

WHITE MAN   [*In fake reconciliation to* FRED] All right!—All right!—All right! Don't make me hurt you!

[FRED *recognizes this as a surrender and finally stops.*]

All right—since you say you're sick, I'm letting you off light this time—but from now on, boy, you'd better watch your step around me—you hear?

[*He looks around at the* SLAVES, *who are still working as if nothing had happened.*]

Now—get on back to work.

[*He looks around, not knowing what else to do—or say—and then leaves. As soon as he clears, the* SLAVES *leave the machine and run to* FRED.]

BLACK MAN   [*With pride and happiness*] Man, oh, man, that was something!

BLACK WOMAN   You whipped ol' Covey to a fare-thee-well!

BLACK MAN   I ain't never seen nothing like that in all my life!

BLACK WOMAN   [*Seeing* FRED *wobble*] How do you feel?

FRED   [*Still winded, but proud, nonetheless, of his accomplishments*] I'm still a little weak, but I'm all right—

BLACK WOMAN   Here, sit down and rest yourself.

[*She takes* FRED *by the arm, but suddenly he is not as tired as he thought.*]

FRED   [*Freeing himself*] Thank you, but I feel all right—no, I feel more than all right—I feel fine—I feel—

[*He tries to find the right word for it.*]

I feel—*free*—I *am* free!—I'm FREE!

[BLACK MAN *and* BLACK WOMAN *look at each other; perhaps* FRED *is losing his reason.*]

BLACK MAN   Fred, son, are you sure you feel all right?

FRED   Of course I feel all right—I'm free—I am free!

[BLACK MAN *and* BLACK WOMAN *are as saddened as they are confused.*]

BLACK WOMAN   Lord, have mercy—

BLACK MAN   Fred, son—

FRED What I'm trying to explain is: I know I am still in
bondage, like everybody else—I got to work and slave
and take hard times, like everybody else. But I ain't
scared now, and that makes me free! I am just as
good, just as worthy, just as free as any other soul
that God ever made. It's just a feeling right now,
and that's all it's gonna be until I make my escape—
nothing but a feeling, but it's the most important
feeling in the world! You know what I mean?

FRED *and* SLAVES

> *Don't you let nobody turn you round*
> *Turn you round*
> *Turn you round*
> *Don't you let nobody turn you round*
> *Keep the straight and the narrow way*
>
> *Ain't gonna let nobody turn me round*
> *Turn me round*
> *Turn me round*
> *Ain't gonna let nobody turn me round*
> *Keep the straight and the narrow way*

[*They continue to hum melody as the set is changed.*]

Scene Five

[*In one corner of the stage is the representation of the hulk of a wooden ship. There* FRED *is busy at work caulking and painting the hull.* FRED *talks as he works.*]

FRED   [*To audience*] Covey never tried to whip me again, and my master, Thomas Auld, decided that I was incorrigible—that it was dangerous to keep me around the other slaves, and finally sent me back to his brother Hugh, in Baltimore, just where I wanted to be to make my escape—but how?

[WHITE BOY *enters, dressed as a shipfitter. He inspects* FRED's *work.*]

WHITE BOY   You're a good caulker, Fred; you're fast and

70

you're thorough, the best I've got. Tell your master I'm very pleased.

FRED   I'll do that, sir.

WHITE BOY   And here's your wages for the week.

[*He counts out some bills and silver into* FRED'*s hand.*]

FREC   Thank you, sir.

[*He exits.* FRED *counts the money, an exercise which makes him angry.*]

FRED   I *was* a good caulker; I worked hard and was paid good wages—every cent of which I had to turn over to Master Hugh. He was at home, waiting for me to come and put these nine dollars into his hands.

[*We hear a harmonica playing offstage.* BLACK MAN, BLACK WOMAN, *and* BLACK BOY *bring on several chairs. They are all dressed neatly as becomes free Negroes, which is what they are.*]

Let him wait! Tonight there was a meeting of the East Baltimore Improvement Society, an organization made up of free Negroes who had let me attend their meetings, although I was, myself, still a slave.

[FRED *steps into the meeting, finds a seat beside* BLACK WOMAN, *who looks at him with a warm but shy smile.*]

COMPANY
            I know my name's

> *Been written down*
> *I know my name's*
> *Been written down*
> *Upon the wall*
> *Been written down*
> *Upon the wall of heaven*
> *Been written down*

FRED We practiced reading and writing and discussed the news sent to us by the abolitionists. I made friends here who became very important to me. Usually the news was good, but sometimes it was bad.

[BLACK MAN, *as president of the society, is addressing the group.*]

BLACK MAN —So forged passes are no longer safe.

FRED Why not?

BLACK MAN The patrollers are too watchful, and it's just too dangerous. But Brother Mentor is to be commended for lending his free papers to a black brother and thus helping him to escape from bondage.

[BLACK BOY, *as Mentor, accepts the congratulations of the group.*]

FRED Excuse me, Brother Mentor, but just how does that work?

BLACK BOY My free papers carry a written description of me—my age, weight, height, the color of my eyes, and so forth.

BLACK MAN   Brother Horace looked enough like Brother Mentor to fit the description, so—

BLACK BOY   So he got on the train here in Baltimore, showed the conductor my papers, and went on through.

FRED   But suppose they had found out that he wasn't you.

BLACK BOY   Well—they would have brought him back and put me in jail.

[*Everybody reacts to the ever-present danger that lies in what they are doing.*]

BLACK MAN   [*Snapping them out of it*] But, thank God, they didn't find out.

BLACK BOY   Mr. President, I move we adjourn so we can get to the camp meeting.

BLACK MAN   So be it, Brother Mentor. Sister Anna, will you join us?

BLACK WOMAN   [*Glancing shyly at* FRED] I'd like to, but— maybe I better not.

BLACK MAN   Well—Brother Fred, will we see you next week?

FRED   I'll be here, all right.

BLACK MAN   [*Gives them a kindly but knowing look.*] Well—er—

[*He exits.* BLACK WOMAN *then hesitates and starts off.* FRED *stops her.*]

FRED   Miss Anna?

73

BLACK WOMAN   [*Shyly*] Yes?

FRED   The society has meant a lot to me—I wouldn't miss a meeting for anything in the world.

BLACK WOMAN   Neither would I—Frederick.

FRED   I've learned so much—the books, the talk, the debates—but, most of all, I come because of you.

[**BLACK WOMAN** *is too shy to make any response, but she is deeply affected.*]

You are not a slave like I am, Anna—

BLACK WOMAN   No, my parents bought their freedom just before I was born.

FRED   If I was free—like you and all the others in the society—would you marry me?

BLACK WOMAN   Oh, yes, Frederick, yes!

[**FRED** *can scarcely conceal his joy.*]

FRED   I *will* be free, Anna, just like Brother Mentor—free, and when I am, Anna, Anna—

BLACK WOMAN   Fred, shouldn't you be getting on home? You told me how your master waits for you each Saturday evening to come and give him your money—

FRED   Let him wait! Come on, Anna, let's catch the wagon before it leaves for the camp meeting.

[*They exit singing.*]

BLACK WOMAN

> *I know your name*

FRED

> *Been written down*

BLACK WOMAN

> *I'm sure your name*

FRED

> *Been written down*
> *Have you seen my name?*

BLACK WOMAN

> *Been written down*

FRED

> *Upon the wall of heaven*

BLACK WOMAN *and* FRED

> *Been written down*

[FRED *and* BLACK WOMAN *rush off.*]

[*From the opposite side a cutout of the Auld house in Baltimore is pushed on.* WHITE MAN, *as Hugh Auld, and* WHITE WOMAN, *as Sophia Auld, enter.*]

WHITE MAN   [*Agitated, pacing*] Where is he—where the hell is he?

WHITE WOMAN   He's never been this late before. Perhaps those white caulkers have hurt him again.

WHITE MAN   Not as much as I am going to hurt him.

WHITE WOMAN   [*Looking off*] Hugh, here he comes!

WHITE MAN   [*Following her gaze*] I'll kill him—I'll break his neck—I'll sell him down the river! I'll—

[FRED *enters.*]

Boy, where have you been?

FRED   I got your money, Master Hugh, got it right here.

WHITE MAN   You're late.

FRED   I'm sorry, sir.

[*He hands money over to* WHITE MAN, *who counts it.*]

If you let me off this time I'll give you an extra day's pay next Saturday.

WHITE MAN   Extra day's pay—where you gonna get the money from? You ain't stealing, are you?

FRED   I found another job—a place where they'll let me work at night. That way I can make extra money—if you'll let me.

WHITE MAN   [*Very much interested*] Extra money, eh—Well, now, Fred, I'm pleased, I really am. Extra money for me and your mistress!

WHITE WOMAN   Oh, Fred, that is so wonderful! God is surely going to bless you—

WHITE MAN   Here's a dime—a ten-cent piece. Now you run along and buy yourself a pretty, you hear?

[WHITE MAN *and* WHITE WOMAN *start off, but* FRED *stops them.*]

FRED   What I had in mind was—well, some masters let their slaves buy themselves free with the extra money they make, and—that's what I'd like to do.

WHITE WOMAN   Why, Fred, whatever's got into you? Haven't we always tried to treat you like a son?

FRED   I'm not your son, I'm your slave, and—

WHITE MAN   The answer is no! You are free to work extra if you want to, and I might even let you keep some of what you earn, but every cent you make belongs to me, every penny—is that clear?

WHITE WOMAN   You are a gift to me, Fred, a personal gift to me from my father!

WHITE MAN   And that's enough of that freedom talk!

[WHITE MAN *and* WHITE WOMAN *exit.*]

FRED   Well, if you won't let me work for my freedom I sure ain't gonna work for you!

[*Hurls dime offstage at them.*]

I'm going!

[*Tambourine indicates passage of time.* FRED *turns and whispers offstage.*]

Anna!

BLACK WOMAN   [*Enters, quickly and surreptitiously.*] Fred—

FRED   Come with me, Anna, you and me, let's make a run for it, you and me.

BLACK WOMAN   Fred, you could be killed if—

FRED   Let them kill me, kill me, kill me! And get it over with!

BLACK WOMAN   Fred, love, I know how you feel, but—does your Master know you are gone?

FRED   No—he still thinks I'm out working on a ship making money for him.

BLACK WOMAN   Go back, Fred—

FRED   What!

BLACK WOMAN   Go back before he finds out you're missing and puts the Sheriff on you—

FRED   No, Anna, I'm leaving—one way or the other—

BLACK WOMAN   How can you leave? You have no money, no free papers to show the conductor—they'll catch you, Fred, and kill you, or sell you down the river.

FRED   Let them catch me, let them kill me—I don't care any more.

BLACK WOMAN   But I do, Fred, I care—

[FRED *looks into her face, loving her, and more miserable in his love now than ever before.*]

FRED   Oh, Anna—Anna—Anna!

[*She holds him close in her arms.*]

BLACK WOMAN   I know, I know, I know—Fred, I have some money—

FRED   What?

BLACK WOMAN   I have some money I've been saving—I want you to take it.

FRED   [*Groaning*] Anna—

BLACK WOMAN   Listen to me: take nine dollars and give it to your master. Beg him to forgive you—do anything, say anything, so that he won't be suspicious.

[*She pulls a knotted handkerchief from her bosom and forces it into his hands.*]

The rest of it will be for your escape. It's not much—but it's all I got, and, Fred—

[WHITE WOMAN's *voice—as* ANNA's *mistress calls to her from offstage*]

WHITE WOMAN   Anna! Anna, what's keeping you out there so long?

BLACK WOMAN   [*Calling off*] Coming, Miss Sarah—

[*Back to* FRED] Mentor, the sailor, is back in town. He wants to see us. Tonight.

WHITE WOMAN   [*Offstage*] Anna!

BLACK WOMAN   Coming, Miss Sarah!

[*To* FRED] I'll be there—

[*She exits.* FRED *looks off after her. He then opens the knotted handkerchief and takes out a small clump of bills. He straightens them out, then looks off after*

79

BLACK WOMAN *for a beat, then runs off.* WHITE MAN, *as Hugh Auld, enters, talking to* WHITE BOY, *as the Sheriff.* WHITE WOMAN, *as Sophia Auld, follows the two in a state of agitation.*]

WHITE MAN —He answers to the name of Fred. He's twenty, twenty-one years old, tall and well-built. Woulda been a good slave except that my wife, Sophia, helped him to learn to read.

WHITE BOY Yeah, that'll ruin 'em every time.

WHITE WOMAN Sheriff, if only I had known—

WHITE MAN But ruined or not, he's still my property, and I want him back—I'll even offer a reward.

WHITE BOY When did you miss him—I mean, when did you see him last?

WHITE MAN Well, the other night he—

WHITE WOMAN [*Looking off*] Hugh, Hugh, here he comes now!

[FRED *enters. She crosses to meet him.*]

Fred—Fred, where have you been?

FRED I'm sorry, Miz Sophia.

WHITE BOY Is this the nigger you talking about?

WHITE MAN It's him, all right. Where in tarnation have you been, boy?

FRED I been working, Master Hugh.

WHITE MAN   Working? I didn't arrange with anybody to hire you out.

FRED   I did it myself. Went to Old Man Carter and told him you sent me, so he took me on. Here's the money—

[FRED *offers the money.* WHITE MAN *greedily snatches it out of his hand and starts counting.*]

WHITE BOY   Well, seems like everything's gonna be all right.

WHITE WOMAN   Oh, yes, Sheriff, our Fred didn't run away after all—but thank you ever so much for coming over.

WHITE BOY   Consider it a privilege, ma'am. Good-by, Mr. Auld.

[*But* WHITE MAN, *counting the money a second time in miserly glee, has already hurried off.*]

WHITE BOY   Good day, ma'am.

[*To* FRED] You got a good master and mistress here, boy—I hope you appreciate that fact.

FRED   Oh, I do, Mr. Sheriff; Master Hugh and Mistress Sophia are the best white folks in all this world, and I love 'em.

WHITE BOY   Make sure you do.

[*He exits.* WHITE WOMAN *turns to Fred and leads him off.*]

WHITE WOMAN   I just knowed that you were too fine, too decent, too intelligent to run off from your master.

FRED   Run off from you, Miz Sophia, and from Mr. Hugh—
        never!

        [*They exit.*]

        [BLACK WOMAN, *as Anna, and* FRED *enter. They are
        met by* BLACK BOY, *as Mentor, the sailor, who is carry-
        ing a package.*]

FRED   [*To* BLACK BOY] What's that?

BLACK BOY   For you to wear.

        [*He opens the carton.* FRED *takes out a sailor suit and
        begins hurriedly to get into it.*]

        But don't buy your ticket until you get on the train.

FRED   Why not?

BLACK BOY   The ticket seller might recognize you. But on
        the train there's usually a crowd, the conductor will
        be busy, and maybe he won't notice.

BLACK WOMAN   Maybe won't notice what?

BLACK BOY   The description on my seaman's papers don't
        resemble Fred at all.

        [FRED *takes the papers and looks at them. His face
        becomes worried, but he makes a decision.*]

FRED   They'll do—they'll have to do.

        [*He puts on his sailor hat, turns and shakes hands
        with* BLACK BOY.]

        You've been a brother—a true brother. I'll send these
        papers back to you the usual way.

BLACK BOY [*Nods his head.*] Good luck.

[*He exits.* FRED *turns to* BLACK WOMAN.]

FRED Anna.

BLACK WOMAN Fred.

[*They embrace.* BLACK WOMAN *pulls away.*]

You'd better go.

FRED I'll write you as soon as I can, but I'm taking a new name for myself, just in case someone else reads my letters to you. I think I'll make it Douglass—Frederick Douglass.

BLACK WOMAN [*Memorizing*] Frederick Douglass.

FRED I'll send for you as soon as I get settled, and then we'll be married.

BLACK WOMAN I'll wait—but hurry.

[FRED *kisses her again and leaves. She stands and watches him.*]

[*The set is rearranged to suggest seats on a train.*

WHITE WOMAN, BLACK MAN, *and* BLACK BOY *are passengers seated on the train. The voice of* WHITE MAN, *the conductor, is heard.*]

WHITE MAN All aboard!

[*Sound effects of train whistle, etc., suggest that the train has begun to move.* FRED, *dressed as a sailor, enters at the last minute and sits near the other blacks. No sooner has he settled than* WHITE BOY, *dressed as a Baltimore businessman, enters from the opposite direction. He starts toward a seat near* WHITE WOMAN, *but stops when he sees* FRED. *He stands for a long moment, as if trying to place him.*]

WHITE BOY   Hey, sailor boy—don't I know you?

[FRED *does not answer.* WHITE BOY *finally passes on to sit beside* WHITE WOMAN, *still looking at* FRED. *He speaks to* WHITE WOMAN.]

You know, I could swear I know that boy.

WHITE WOMAN   If you do, you beat me—all the darkies look alike to me.

WHITE BOY   That's true, but—

[*Suddenly, to* FRED] Hey, boy, did you ever live up near St. Michael's?

[FRED *begins to sweat, but does not answer.* WHITE MAN *enters and starts down the aisle.*]

WHITE MAN   All tickets, please.

[*He comes to the place where the blacks are clustered.*]

Let me see your papers—your free papers.

[*The blacks all show their papers.* WHITE MAN *comes to* FRED *and first takes his money.* WHITE BOY *rises from his seat, saunters over, and stands above* FRED.]

WHITE BOY   [*As if he suddenly recognized him*] Yeah—I

know this boy, conductor—I know him.

FRED   [*Wiping his face*] Of course you know me, sir, I sailed on a packet out of Philadelphia.

WHITE BOY   Out of Philadelphia?

FRED   Well, not only Philadelphia—I've shipped out of every port on the eastern seaboard—Savannah, Charleston. New York—I'm sure we met on one of my ships, sir.

WHITE BOY   Well, if that's the case, why didn't you answer when I spoke to you? What are you hiding for?

FRED   [*Suddenly friendly and jovial*] Oh, I'm not hiding. It's just that—

WHITE MAN   You have your seaman's papers?

FRED   Yes, sir. Here they are right here.

[*He reaches inside his pocket for papers, but meanwhile continues his bluff.*]

You see, sir, although I'm a sailor—a darn good sailor —I still get seasick. And one time—[*He is still stalling.*] one time, I'm ashamed to admit it, sir, one time I ran to the rail to settle my stomach and fell overboard! All the people had a right good laugh at my expense.

WHITE BOY   [*Trying hard to figure it*] And where'd you say all this happened?

FRED   Charleston Harbor, don't you remember? It whistled up rough with a high wind to starboard, and breakers coming in fast and white o'er the gunnels. I grabbed at the bosun and missed—couldn't swim, either, so there I was, if you remember, sir, damn near drowned.

[FRED *is laughing uncontrollably as he puts the false seaman's papers into* WHITE MAN'*s hand. Before* WHITE MAN *can examine the papers,* FRED *pulls him into the story.*]

You should have seen this black sailorman, conductor, flapping around like a catfish in a hot skillet.

[WHITE MAN *laughs, then has another go at the papers.* FRED *grabs his elbow as he continues the recital.*]

I swear—first time ever in my life—I seen somebody black as me—turn blue!

[*This is a joke that both* WHITE MAN *and* WHITE BOY *can appreciate. They double over in laughter, and while they are howling,* FRED *deftly lifts his papers from* WHITE MAN'*s hands, and puts them back into his pocket.* WHITE MAN *and* WHITE BOY *keep laughing as they leave* FRED *and move on up the aisle.* WHITE MAN *has a funny story of his own.*]

WHITE MAN   That reminds me of this ol' nigger man, Uncle Somby, who used to take us boys fishing. Now, Uncle Somby was as fine a darky as you ever wanted to see, but he was blind in one eye and couldn't see much out of the other—but too proud to admit it. So one night ol' Somby—

[*The* COMPANY *freezes.* FRED *rises and steps out of scene to address audience.*]

86

FRED On the third day of September, 1838, I left my chains behind and succeeded in reaching New York without any further interruptions.

[*The cast begins to hum the melody to "Freedom Land" as* FRED *continues.*]

The first thing I did was to send for Anna.

[BLACK WOMAN *runs in, carrying bag, dressed in traveling clothes. She and* FRED *embrace warmly.*]

Come on.

BLACK WOMAN But, Fred, where are we going?

FRED To find Reverend Pennington, so you and I—two free people—can get married!

[*The cast rearrange themselves to suggest a parlor.* FRED *and* BLACK WOMAN *stand before* BLACK MAN, *the minister.* BLACK BOY, WHITE MAN, WHITE BOY, *and* WHITE WOMAN *are also present as abolitionist friends.*]

BLACK MAN I now pronounce you man and wife.

[BLACK WOMAN *comes down front.*]

BLACK WOMAN [*To audience*] Frederick Douglass went on to become one of the greatest orators America has ever produced.

[WHITE WOMAN *joins her.*]

WHITE WOMAN [*To audience*] Later, in order to reach more people, he published an abolitionist newspaper in Rochester, New York—*The North Star.*

[BLACK MAN *comes down.*]

BLACK MAN   [*To audience*] He wrote several books about his life, and many books were written about him.

[*The others come down.*]

WHITE MAN   He was an adviser to President Abraham Lincoln.

BLACK BOY   He persuaded Lincoln to let the black man fight in the Civil War for his own freedom.

WHITE BOY   He became U.S. Ambassador to Haiti, the first black man to hold a diplomatic post—

BLACK WOMAN   —and one of the first to speak for women's rights.

FRED   Frederick Douglass—an extraordinary American.

COMPANY

> *I'm on my way, great God*
> *I'm on my way*
>
> *I'm on my way*
> *To the freedom land*
> *I'm on my way*
> *To the freedom land*
> *I'm on my way*
> *To the freedom land*
> *I'm on my way, great God*
> *I'm on my way*

CURTAIN

Selected Bibliography

Brackett, Jeffrey. *The Negro in Maryland: The Study of the Institution Slavery.* Freeport, N.Y.: Books for Libraries Press, 1969.

Douglass, Frederick. *Life and Times of Frederick Douglass.* New York: Collier Books, 1892, reprinted, 1962.

Graham, Shirley. *There Once Was a Slave, The Heroic Story of Frederick Douglass.* New York: Julian Messner, Inc., 1947.

Holland, Frederick May. *Frederick Douglass: The Colored Orator.* New York: Funk and Wagnalls Co., 1895.

Williams, Eric. *Capitalism and Slavery.* Chapel Hill, N.C.: University of North Carolina Press, 1944.

About the author

OSSIE DAVIS is the well-known actor and playwright. He wrote and performed in the comedy *Purlie Victorious* and directed the movie *Cotton Comes to Harlem*. He has made many television appearances, has starred in numerous films and plays, and has long been an activist in the cause of human rights.